I am so *prosperous*

Sky Hawk

Published by Uiri Press 2017
First edition, first printing

Design and writing © 2017 Sky Hawk

All rights reserved. No part of this book may be reproduced or transmitted in any form or by any means, including but not limited to information storage and retrieval systems, electronic, mechanical, photocopy, recording, etc. without written permission from the copyright holder.

ISBN; 978-0-9979051-3-7

Dedication

To all the healthy examples of prosperity
and success in this world.
Thank you

How To Use This Book

This is a 56 day journal that is focused on bringing more prosperity in your life!
Take the baseline survey that follows on the next few pages to get an idea of where you are in your thought
process around prosperity right now.

1. Read the quote and take some time to contemplate upon it. I like to use these for a daily focus.

2. Write about how you are already prosperous. What abilities do you *already* have that make you successful? What are you thankful for in your life that relates to prosperity?

3. Write out your prosperity plan. This is something you will do daily because as you write it you will begin to refine your plan and get more insight as to what you really want. And it will keep you focused upon it. It also helps to make a clearer picture in your head. As each day goes by feel yourself getting excited about it.

4. On the first day of the week you will write out the big action steps you need to take toward bringing your plan into reality. Then you will write daily about the action steps you actually took that day.

5. Write about your bliss points. This is something that makes you happy and joyful. When we are in a joyful state we can imprint our brains with new information. (Example; our wonderful prosperity plan)

6. Every seventh day there will be a weekly review.

Think about people you admire, this can be friends, family, world leaders, wealthy people, even fictional characters.
Answer the following questions about these people...

People I admire the most are _____

Here are their admirable qualities? _____

How can I emulate them? _____

What is it that I want to achieve/ create/ aspire to/ contribute? _____

What am I capable of doing? What makes me unique? _____

What excites me? _____
_____
_____
_____

What are my core values? _____
_____
_____
_____

What are my strengths? _____
_____
_____
_____

How much money do I need to accomplish what I want to achieve? _____
_____

When I get this money how will I manage it? _____
_____
_____
_____

How do I see money right now? Is it a friend or foe? Is it helpful or a burden? _____
_____
_____

How will my life look when I become prosperous? _____
_____
_____
_____
_____

Vision Time
Draw a picture of what you will be doing when you are prosperous. Or paste in a photo.

Week 1

Date _____

How am I already prosperous? What abilities do I have to contribute to my prosperity?

_____
_____
_____
_____
_____

My prosperity plan!! Write down what you plan to accomplish this week based on what you said you wanted to achieve.

_____
_____
_____
_____
_____
_____
_____
_____

Big actions I need to take this week in accordance with my plan.

_____
_____
_____
_____
_____
_____
_____

Small action steps I took today

1. _____
_____
_____

2. _____
_____
_____

3. _____
_____
_____

action taking meter

I did everything I set out to do

⋮

I didn't do anything

> Success is no accident. It is hard work, perseverance, learning, studying, sacrifice and most of all, love of what you are doing or learning to do.
> Pele

Bliss Points
When we focus ourselves on finding our bliss, it is easier to get into alignment with prosperity. What did you do today that brought you bliss?

_____
_____
_____
_____
_____
_____
_____

Week 1

Date _____

How am I already prosperous? What am I thankful for in my life right now?

_____
_____
_____
_____
_____

My prosperity plan!! Write down what you plan to accomplish this week based on what you said you waned to achieve. (Yes, you must write it again. Repetition drives it deeper into your brain. Refine the details if necessary.)

_____
_____
_____
_____
_____
_____
_____
_____
_____
_____

> Put your heart, mind, and soul into even your smallest acts. This is the secret of success.
>
> Swami Sivananda

Small action steps I took today

1. _____

2. _____

3. _____

action taking meter

I did everything I set out to do

I didn't do anything

Bliss Points
When we focus ourselves on finding our bliss, it is easier to get into alignment with prosperity. What did you do today that brought you bliss?

_____

Week 1

Date _____

How am I already prosperous? What am I thankful for in my life right now?

_____
_____
_____
_____
_____

My prosperity plan!! Write down what you plan to accomplish this week based on what you said you waned to achieve. (Yes, you must write it again. Repetition drives it deeper into your brain. Refine the details if necessary.)

_____
_____
_____
_____
_____
_____
_____
_____
_____
_____
_____

> A strong, positive self-image is the best possible preparation for success.
>
> Joyce Brothers

Small action steps I took today

1. _____
_____
_____

2. _____
_____
_____

3. _____
_____
_____
_____

action taking meter

I did everything I set out to do

I didn't do anything

Bliss Points
When we focus ourselves on finding our bliss, it is easier to get into alignment with prosperity. What did you do today that brought you bliss?

_____
_____
_____
_____
_____
_____
_____
_____
_____
_____
_____

Week 1

Date _____

How am I already prosperous? What am I thankful for in my life right now?

_____
_____
_____
_____
_____

My prosperity plan!! Write down what you plan to accomplish this week based on what you said you waned to achieve. (Yes, you must write it again. Repetition drives it deeper into your brain. Refine the details if necessary.)

_____
_____
_____
_____
_____
_____
_____
_____
_____
_____

> Success is not final, failure is not fatal: it is the courage to continue that counts.
>
> Winston Churchill

Small action steps I took today

1. _____

_____

_____

2. _____

_____

_____

3. _____

_____

_____

_____

_____

action taking meter

I did everything I set out to do

I didn't do anything

Bliss Points

When we focus ourselves on finding our bliss, it is easier to get into alignment with prosperity. What did you do today that brought you bliss?

_____

_____

_____

_____

_____

_____

_____

_____

_____

_____

Week 1

Date _____

How am I already prosperous? What am I thankful for in my life right now?

_____
_____
_____
_____
_____

My prosperity plan!! Write down what you plan to accomplish this week based on what you said you waned to achieve. (Yes, you must write it again. Repetition drives it deeper into your brain. Refine the details if necessary.)

_____
_____
_____
_____
_____
_____
_____
_____
_____

> Success is the result of perfection, hard work, learning from failure, loyalty, and persistence.
>
> Colin Powell

Small action steps I took today

1. _____
_____
_____

2. _____
_____
_____

3. _____
_____
_____
_____
_____

action taking meter

I did everything I set out to do

I didn't do anything

Bliss Points
When we focus ourselves on finding our bliss, it is easier to get into alignment with prosperity. What did you do today that brought you bliss?

_____
_____
_____
_____
_____
_____
_____
_____
_____
_____
_____

Week 1

Date _____

How am I already prosperous? What am I thankful for in my life right now?

_____
_____
_____
_____

My prosperity plan!! Write down what you plan to accomplish this week based on what you said you waned to achieve. (Yes, you must write it again. Repetition drives it deeper into your brain. Refine the details if necessary.)

_____
_____
_____
_____
_____
_____
_____
_____
_____
_____
_____
_____

> Success is not the key to happiness. Happiness is the key to success.
> If you love what you are doing, you will be successful.
>
> Albert Schweitzer

Small action steps I took today

1. _____
_____
_____

2. _____
_____
_____

3. _____
_____
_____
_____

action taking meter

I did everything I set out to do

I didn't do anything

Bliss Points
When we focus ourselves on finding our bliss, it is easier to get into alignment with prosperity. What did you do today that brought you bliss?

_____
_____
_____
_____
_____
_____
_____
_____
_____
_____
_____

What a week! I love my prosperity journal.

Write down the difference you notice in your life as you have been focused on
prosperity.

> Try not to become a man
> of success,
> but rather
> try to become a
> man of value.
>
> Albert Einstein

**** *Blissful Actions* ****

Date _____

Weekly Check-In

Have I been staying in alignment with my values during my prosperity practice? Have I been using my strengths to the best of my ability? Have I been seeking help when I need it? Am I staying authentic to myself?

_____
_____
_____
_____
_____
_____
_____
_____
_____
_____
_____
_____
_____
_____
_____
_____
_____
_____

prosperity meter

Life's great, but..I'm ready for more.

I am thriving!! Life is blooming.

Week 2

Date _____

How am I already prosperous? What abilities do I have to contribute to my prosperity?

_____
_____
_____
_____
_____
_____
_____

My prosperity plan!! Write down what you plan to accomplish this week based on what you said you wanted to achieve.

_____
_____
_____
_____
_____
_____
_____
_____

Big actions I need to take this week in accordance with my plan.

_____
_____
_____
_____
_____
_____
_____

Small action steps I took today

1. _____

2. _____

3. _____

action taking meter

I did everything I set out to do

I didn't do anything

> Happiness lies in the joy of achievement and the thrill of creative effort.
> Franklin D. Roosevelt

Bliss Points

When we focus ourselves on finding our bliss, it is easier to get into alignment with prosperity. What did you do today that brought you bliss?

_____
_____
_____
_____
_____
_____
_____

Week 2

Date _____

How am I already prosperous? What am I thankful for in my life right now?

_____
_____
_____
_____
_____

My prosperity plan!! Write down what you plan to accomplish this week based on what you said you waned to achieve. (Yes, you must write it again. Repetition drives it deeper into your brain. Refine the details if necessary.)

_____
_____
_____
_____
_____
_____
_____
_____
_____
_____

> Coming together is a beginning;
> keeping together is progress;
> working together
> is success.
>
> Henry Ford

Small action steps I took today

1. _____

2. _____

3. _____

action taking meter

I did everything I set out to do

I didn't do anything

Bliss Points
When we focus ourselves on finding our bliss, it is easier to get into alignment with prosperity. What did you do today that brought you bliss?

Week 2

Date _____

How am I already prosperous? What am I thankful for in my life right now?

_____
_____
_____
_____
_____

My prosperity plan!! Write down what you plan to accomplish this week based on what you said you waned to achieve. (Yes, you must write it again. Repetition drives it deeper into your brain. Refine the details if necessary.)

_____
_____
_____
_____
_____
_____
_____
_____
_____
_____
_____

> The price of success is hard work, dedication to the job at hand, and the determination that whether we win or lose, we have applied the best of ourselves to the task at hand.
>
> — Vince Lombardi

Small action steps I took today

1. _____

2. _____

3. _____

action taking meter

I did everything I set out to do

I didn't do anything

Bliss Points
When we focus ourselves on finding our bliss, it is easier to get into alignment with prosperity. What did you do today that brought you bliss?

Week 2

Date _____

How am I already prosperous? What am I thankful for in my life right now?

_____
_____
_____
_____
_____

My prosperity plan!! Write down what you plan to accomplish this week based on what you said you waned to achieve. (Yes, you must write it again. Repetition drives it deeper into your brain. Refine the details if necessary.)

_____
_____
_____
_____
_____
_____
_____
_____
_____
_____
_____

> All you need in this life is ignorance and confidence, and then success is sure.
>
> Mark Twain

Small action steps I took today

1. _____
_____
_____

2. _____
_____
_____

3. _____
_____
_____
_____
_____

action taking meter

I did everything I set out to do

I didn't do anything

Bliss Points
When we focus ourselves on finding our bliss, it is easier to get into alignment with prosperity. What did you do today that brought you bliss?

_____
_____
_____
_____
_____
_____
_____
_____
_____
_____
_____
_____

Week 2

Date _____

How am I already prosperous? What am I thankful for in my life right now?

_____
_____
_____
_____
_____

My prosperity plan!! Write down what you plan to accomplish this week based on what you said you waned to achieve. (Yes, you must write it again. Repetition drives it deeper into your brain. Refine the details if necessary.)

_____
_____
_____
_____
_____
_____
_____
_____
_____
_____
_____

> Patience, persistence and perspiration make an unbeatable combination for success.
>
> Napoleon Hill

Small action steps I took today

1. _____
_____
_____

2. _____
_____
_____

3. _____
_____
_____
_____
_____

action taking meter

I did everything I set out to do

I didn't do anything

Bliss Points
When we focus ourselves on finding our bliss, it is easier to get into alignment with prosperity. What did you do today that brought you bliss?

_____
_____
_____
_____
_____
_____
_____
_____
_____
_____
_____
_____

Week 2

Date _____

How am I already prosperous? What am I thankful for in my life right now?

_____
_____
_____
_____
_____

My prosperity plan!! Write down what you plan to accomplish this week based on what you said you waned to achieve. (Yes, you must write it again. Repetition drives it deeper into your brain. Refine the details if necessary.)

_____
_____
_____
_____
_____
_____
_____
_____
_____

> Success consists of going from failure to failure without loss of enthusiasm.
>
> Winston Churchill

Small action steps I took today

1. _____

2. _____

3. _____

action taking meter

I did everything I set out to do

I didn't do anything

Bliss Points
When we focus ourselves on finding our bliss, it is easier to get into alignment with prosperity. What did you do today that brought you bliss?

What a week! I love my prosperity journal.

Write down the difference you notice in your life as you have been focused on prosperity.

> Character cannot be developed in ease and quiet. Only through experience of trial and suffering can the soul be strengthened, ambition inspired, and success achieved.
> Helen Keller

**** *Blissful Actions* ****

Date _____

Weekly Check-In

Have I been staying in alignment with my values during my prosperity practice? Have I been using my strengths to the best of my ability? Have I been seeking help when I need it? Am I staying authentic to myself?

_____
_____
_____
_____
_____
_____
_____
_____
_____
_____
_____
_____
_____
_____
_____
_____
_____
_____
_____

prosperity meter

Life's great, but..I'm ready for more.

I am thriving!! Life is blooming.

Week 3

Date _____

How am I already prosperous? What abilities do I have to contribute to my prosperity?

_____
_____
_____
_____
_____
_____

My prosperity plan!! Write down what you plan to accomplish this week based on what you said you wanted to achieve.

_____
_____
_____
_____
_____
_____
_____
_____
_____

Big actions I need to take this week in accordance with my plan.

_____
_____
_____
_____
_____
_____
_____

Small action steps I took today

1. _____
_____

2. _____
_____

3. _____
_____

action taking meter

I did everything I set out to do

I didn't do anything

> Success is where preparation and opportunity meet.
>
> Bobby Unser

Bliss Points
When we focus ourselves on finding our bliss, it is easier to get into alignment with prosperity. What did you do today that brought you bliss?

_____
_____
_____
_____
_____
_____
_____

Week 3

Date _____

How am I already prosperous? What am I thankful for in my life right now?

_____
_____
_____
_____
_____

My prosperity plan!! Write down what you plan to accomplish this week based on what you said you waned to achieve. (Yes, you must write it again. Repetition drives it deeper into your brain. Refine the details if necessary.)

_____
_____
_____
_____
_____
_____
_____
_____
_____

> Success is simple.
> Do what's right,
> the right way,
> at the right time.
>
> Arnold H. Glasow

Small action steps I took today

1. _____

2. _____

3. _____

action taking meter

I did everything I set out to do

I didn't do anything

Bliss Points
When we focus ourselves on finding our bliss, it is easier to get into alignment with prosperity. What did you do today that brought you bliss?

Week 3

Date _____

How am I already prosperous? What am I thankful for in my life right now?

_____
_____
_____
_____
_____

My prosperity plan!! Write down what you plan to accomplish this week based on what you said you waned to achieve. (Yes, you must write it again. Repetition drives it deeper into your brain. Refine the details if necessary.)

_____
_____
_____
_____
_____
_____
_____
_____
_____
_____

> If everyone is moving forward together, then success takes care of itself.
>
> Henry Ford

Small action steps I took today

1. _____
_____
_____

2. _____
_____
_____

3. _____
_____
_____
_____
_____

action taking meter

I did everything I set out to do

⋮

I didn't do anything

Bliss Points
When we focus ourselves on finding our bliss, it is easier to get into alignment with prosperity. What did you do today that brought you bliss?

_____
_____
_____
_____
_____
_____
_____
_____
_____
_____
_____
_____

Week 3

Date _____

How am I already prosperous? What am I thankful for in my life right now?

_____
_____
_____
_____
_____

My prosperity plan!! Write down what you plan to accomplish this week based on what you said you waned to achieve. (Yes, you must write it again. Repetition drives it deeper into your brain. Refine the details if necessary.)

_____
_____
_____
_____
_____
_____
_____
_____
_____
_____
_____

> It's fine to celebrate success but it is more important to heed the lessons of failure.
>
> Bill Gates

Small action steps I took today

1. _____
   _____
   _____

2. _____
   _____
   _____

3. _____
   _____
   _____
   _____
   _____

action taking meter

I did everything I set out to do

⋮

I didn't do anything

Bliss Points
When we focus ourselves on finding our bliss, it is easier to get into alignment with prosperity. What did you do today that brought you bliss?

_____
_____
_____
_____
_____
_____
_____
_____
_____
_____
_____

Week 3

Date _____

How am I already prosperous? What am I thankful for in my life right now?

_____
_____
_____
_____
_____

My prosperity plan!! Write down what you plan to accomplish this week based on what you said you waned to achieve. (Yes, you must write it again. Repetition drives it deeper into your brain. Refine the details if necessary.)

_____
_____
_____
_____
_____
_____
_____
_____
_____
_____

> Success comes to those who dedicate everything to their passion in life.
>
> A. R. Rahman

Small action steps I took today

1. _____
_____
_____

2. _____
_____
_____

3. _____
_____
_____
_____
_____

action taking meter

I did everything I set out to do

I didn't do anything

Bliss Points
When we focus ourselves on finding our bliss, it is easier to get into alignment with prosperity. What did you do today that brought you bliss?

_____
_____
_____
_____
_____
_____
_____
_____
_____
_____
_____

Week 3

Date _____

How am I already prosperous? What am I thankful for in my life right now?

_____
_____
_____
_____
_____

My prosperity plan!! Write down what you plan to accomplish this week based on what you said you waned to achieve. (Yes, you must write it again. Repetition drives it deeper into your brain. Refine the details if necessary.)

_____
_____
_____
_____
_____
_____
_____
_____
_____
_____

> Success is a journey,
> not a destination.
> The doing is often more important
> than the outcome.
>
> Arthur Ashe

Small action steps I took today

1. _____
_____
_____

2. _____
_____
_____

3. _____
_____
_____
_____

action taking meter

I did everything I set out to do

I didn't do anything

Bliss Points
When we focus ourselves on finding our bliss, it is easier to get into alignment with prosperity. What did you do today that brought you bliss?

_____
_____
_____
_____
_____
_____
_____
_____
_____
_____
_____

What a week! I love my prosperity journal.

Write down the difference you notice in your life as you have been focused on
prosperity.

_____
_____
_____
_____
_____
_____
_____
_____
_____

> Always bear in mind
> that your own
> resolution
> to succeed is more
> important than
> any other.
>
> Abraham Lincoln

**** *Blissful Actions* ****

_____
_____
_____
_____
_____

Date _____

Weekly Check-In

Have I been staying in alignment with my values during my prosperity practice? Have I been using my strengths to the best of my ability? Have I been seeking help when I need it? Am I staying authentic to myself?

_____
_____
_____
_____
_____
_____
_____
_____
_____
_____
_____
_____
_____
_____
_____
_____
_____

prosperity meter

| Life's great, but..I'm ready for more. | | I am thriving!! Life is blooming. |

Week 4

Date _____

How am I already prosperous? What abilities do I have to contribute to my prosperity?

_____
_____
_____
_____
_____
_____

My prosperity plan!! Write down what you plan to accomplish this week based on what you said you wanted to achieve.

_____
_____
_____
_____
_____
_____
_____
_____

Big actions I need to take this week in accordance with my plan.

_____
_____
_____
_____
_____
_____
_____

Small action steps I took today

1. _____
_____
_____

2. _____
_____
_____

3. _____
_____
_____

action taking meter

I did everything I set out to do

I didn't do anything

> Some people dream of success, while other people get up every morning and make it happen.
> Wayne Huizenga

Bliss Points
When we focus ourselves on finding our bliss, it is easier to get into alignment with prosperity. What did you do today that brought you bliss?

_____
_____
_____
_____
_____
_____
_____

Week 4

Date _____

How am I already prosperous? What am I thankful for in my life right now?

_____
_____
_____
_____
_____

My prosperity plan!! Write down what you plan to accomplish this week based on what you said you waned to achieve. (Yes, you must write it again. Repetition drives it deeper into your brain. Refine the details if necessary.)

_____
_____
_____
_____
_____
_____
_____
_____
_____
_____
_____
_____

> Take up one idea. Make that one idea your life - think of it, dream of it, live on that idea. Let the brain, muscles, nerves, every part of your body, be full of that idea, and just leave every other idea alone. This is the way to success.
> Swami Vivekananda

Small action steps I took today

1. _____

2. _____

3. _____

action taking meter

I did everything I set out to do

I didn't do anything

Bliss Points
When we focus ourselves on finding our bliss, it is easier to get into alignment with prosperity. What did you do today that brought you bliss?

Week 4

Date _____

How am I already prosperous? What am I thankful for in my life right now?

_____
_____
_____
_____
_____

My prosperity plan!! Write down what you plan to accomplish this week based on what you said you waned to achieve. (Yes, you must write it again. Repetition drives it deeper into your brain. Refine the details if necessary.)

_____
_____
_____
_____
_____
_____
_____
_____
_____

> Desire is the key to motivation, but it's determination and commitment to an unrelenting pursuit of your goal - a commitment to excellence - that will enable you to attain the success you seek.
> Mario Andretti

Small action steps I took today

1. _____
_____
_____

2. _____
_____
_____

3. _____
_____
_____
_____
_____

action taking meter

I did everything I set out to do

I didn't do anything

Bliss Points
When we focus ourselves on finding our bliss, it is easier to get into alignment with prosperity. What did you do today that brought you bliss?

Week 4

Date _____

How am I already prosperous? What am I thankful for in my life right now?

_____
_____
_____
_____
_____

My prosperity plan!! Write down what you plan to accomplish this week based on what you said you waned to achieve. (Yes, you must write it again. Repetition drives it deeper into your brain. Refine the details if necessary.)

_____
_____
_____
_____
_____
_____
_____
_____
_____
_____
_____
_____

> Think little goals and expect little achievements. Think big goals and win big success.
>
> David Joseph Schwartz

Small action steps I took today

1. _____
_____
_____

2. _____
_____
_____

3. _____
_____
_____
_____
_____

action taking meter

I did everything I set out to do

I didn't do anything

Bliss Points
When we focus ourselves on finding our bliss, it is easier to get into alignment with prosperity. What did you do today that brought you bliss?

_____
_____
_____
_____
_____
_____
_____
_____
_____
_____
_____
_____

Week 4

Date _____

How am I already prosperous? What am I thankful for in my life right now?

_____
_____
_____
_____
_____

My prosperity plan!! Write down what you plan to accomplish this week based on what you said you waned to achieve. (Yes, you must write it again. Repetition drives it deeper into your brain. Refine the details if necessary.)

_____
_____
_____
_____
_____
_____
_____
_____
_____
_____

> My powers are ordinary. Only my application brings me success.
>
> Isaac Newton

Small action steps I took today

1. _____
_____
_____

2. _____
_____
_____

3. _____
_____
_____
_____
_____

action taking meter

I did everything I set out to do

[ ]

I didn't do anything

Bliss Points
When we focus ourselves on finding our bliss, it is easier to get into alignment with prosperity. What did you do today that brought you bliss?

_____
_____
_____
_____
_____
_____
_____
_____
_____
_____
_____

Week 4

Date _____

How am I already prosperous? What am I thankful for in my life right now?

_____
_____
_____
_____
_____

My prosperity plan!! Write down what you plan to accomplish this week based on what you said you waned to achieve. (Yes, you must write it again. Repetition drives it deeper into your brain. Refine the details if necessary.)

_____
_____
_____
_____
_____
_____
_____
_____
_____
_____

> Money won't create success, the freedom to make it will.
>
> Nelson Mandela

Small action steps I took today

1. _____
_____
_____

2. _____
_____
_____

3. _____
_____
_____
_____
_____

action taking meter

I did everything I set out to do

```
..............
. .
. .
. .
. .
. .
. .
. .
. .
. .
. .
. .
. .
..............
```

I didn't do anything

Bliss Points
When we focus ourselves on finding our bliss, it is easier to get into alignment with prosperity. What did you do today that brought you bliss?

_____
_____
_____
_____
_____
_____
_____
_____
_____
_____
_____
_____
_____

What a week! I love my prosperity journal.

Write down the difference you notice in your life as you have been focused on prosperity.

> We were all born with a certain degree of power.
> The key to success is discovering this innate power and using it daily to deal with whatever challenges come our way.
>
> Les Brown

**** *Blissful Actions* ****

Date _____

Weekly Check-In

Have I been staying in alignment with my values during my prosperity practice? Have I been using my strengths to the best of my ability? Have I been seeking help when I need it? Am I staying authentic to myself?

_____
_____
_____
_____
_____
_____
_____
_____
_____
_____
_____
_____
_____
_____
_____
_____
_____
_____
_____
_____

prosperity meter

| Life's great, but..I'm ready for more. | | I am thriving!! Life is blooming. |

Week 5

Date _____

How am I already prosperous? What abilities do I have to contribute to my prosperity?

_____
_____
_____
_____
_____
_____

My prosperity plan!! Write down what you plan to accomplish this week based on what you said you wanted to achieve.

_____
_____
_____
_____
_____
_____
_____
_____

Big actions I need to take this week in accordance with my plan.

_____
_____
_____
_____
_____
_____
_____

Small action steps I took today

1. _____

2. _____

3. _____

action taking meter

I did everything I set out to do

I didn't do anything

> Success does not consist in never making mistakes but in never making the same one a second time.
>
> George Bernard Shaw

Bliss Points
When we focus ourselves on finding our bliss, it is easier to get into alignment with prosperity. What did you do today that brought you bliss?

_____
_____
_____
_____
_____
_____
_____
_____

Week 5

Date _____

How am I already prosperous? What am I thankful for in my life right now?

_____
_____
_____
_____
_____

My prosperity plan!! Write down what you plan to accomplish this week based on what you said you waned to achieve. (Yes, you must write it again. Repetition drives it deeper into your brain. Refine the details if necessary.)

_____
_____
_____
_____
_____
_____
_____
_____
_____
_____
_____

> Before anything else, preparation is the key to success.
>
> Alexander Graham Bell

Small action steps I took today

1. _____
_____
_____

2. _____
_____
_____

3. _____
_____
_____
_____
_____

action taking meter

I did everything I set out to do

I didn't do anything

Bliss Points
When we focus ourselves on finding our bliss, it is easier to get into alignment with prosperity. What did you do today that brought you bliss?

_____
_____
_____
_____
_____
_____
_____
_____
_____
_____
_____

Week 5

Date _____

How am I already prosperous? What am I thankful for in my life right now?

_____
_____
_____
_____

My prosperity plan!! Write down what you plan to accomplish this week based on what you said you waned to achieve. (Yes, you must write it again. Repetition drives it deeper into your brain. Refine the details if necessary.)

> The most important single ingredient in the formula of success is knowing how to get along with people.
>
> Theodore Roosevelt

Small action steps I took today

1. _____

2. _____

3. _____

action taking meter

I did everything I set out to do

I didn't do anything

Bliss Points
When we focus ourselves on finding our bliss, it is easier to get into alignment with prosperity. What did you do today that brought you bliss?

Week 5

Date _____

How am I already prosperous? What am I thankful for in my life right now?

_____
_____
_____
_____
_____

My prosperity plan!! Write down what you plan to accomplish this week based on what you said you waned to achieve. (Yes, you must write it again. Repetition drives it deeper into your brain. Refine the details if necessary.)

_____
_____
_____
_____
_____
_____
_____
_____
_____
_____

> The secret of our success is that we never, never give up.
>
> Wilma Mankiller

Small action steps I took today

1. _____
_____
_____

2. _____
_____
_____

3. _____
_____
_____
_____
_____

action taking meter

I did everything I set out to do

I didn't do anything

Bliss Points
When we focus ourselves on finding our bliss, it is easier to get into alignment with prosperity. What did you do today that brought you bliss?

_____
_____
_____
_____
_____
_____
_____
_____
_____
_____
_____

Week 5

Date _____

How am I already prosperous? What am I thankful for in my life right now?

_____
_____
_____
_____
_____

My prosperity plan!! Write down what you plan to accomplish this week based on what you said you waned to achieve. (Yes, you must write it again. Repetition drives it deeper into your brain. Refine the details if necessary.)

_____
_____
_____
_____
_____
_____
_____
_____
_____
_____

> One important key to success is self-confidence. An important key to self-confidence is preparation.
>
> — Arthur Ashe

Small action steps I took today
1. _____
_____
_____

2. _____
_____
_____

3. _____
_____
_____
_____
_____

action taking meter

I did
everything I
set out to do

I didn't do
anything

Bliss Points
When we focus ourselves on finding our bliss, it is easier to get into alignment with prosperity. What did you do today that brought you bliss?

_____
_____
_____
_____
_____
_____
_____
_____
_____
_____
_____
_____

Week 5

Date_____

How am I already prosperous? What am I thankful for in my life right now?

_____
_____
_____
_____

My prosperity plan!! Write down what you plan to accomplish this week based on what you said you waned to achieve. (Yes, you must write it again. Repetition drives it deeper into your brain. Refine the details if necessary.)

_____
_____
_____
_____
_____
_____
_____
_____
_____
_____
_____

> Success is not a destination, but the road that you're on. Being successful means that you're working hard and walking your walk every day. You can only live your dream by working hard towards it.
> That's living your dream.
> Marlon Wayans

Small action steps I took today

1. _____
   _____
   _____

2. _____
   _____
   _____

3. _____
   _____
   _____
   _____

action taking meter

I did everything I set out to do

I didn't do anything

Bliss Points

When we focus ourselves on finding our bliss, it is easier to get into alignment with prosperity. What did you do today that brought you bliss?

_____
_____
_____
_____
_____
_____
_____
_____
_____
_____
_____

What a week! I love my prosperity journal.

Write down the difference you notice in your life as you have been focused on prosperity.

> Success is peace of mind which is a direct result of self-satisfaction in knowing you did your best to become the best you are capable of becoming.
>
> John Wooden

**** Blissful Actions ****

Date _____

Weekly Check-In

Have I been staying in alignment with my values during my prosperity practice? Have I been using my strengths to the best of my ability? Have I been seeking help when I need it? Am I staying authentic to myself?

_____
_____
_____
_____
_____
_____
_____
_____
_____
_____
_____
_____
_____
_____
_____
_____
_____

prosperity meter

| Life's great, but..I'm ready for more. | | I am thriving!! Life is blooming. |

Week 6

Date _____

How am I already prosperous? What abilities do I have to contribute to my prosperity?

_____
_____
_____
_____
_____
_____

My prosperity plan!! Write down what you plan to accomplish this week based on what you said you wanted to achieve.

_____
_____
_____
_____
_____
_____
_____
_____

Big actions I need to take this week in accordance with my plan.

_____
_____
_____
_____
_____
_____
_____

Small action steps I took today

1. _____
_____
_____

2. _____
_____
_____

3. _____
_____
_____

action taking meter

I did everything I set out to do

I didn't do anything

> It had long since come to my attention that people of accomplishment rarely sat back and let things happen to them. They went out and happened to things.
> Leonardo da Vinci

Bliss Points
When we focus ourselves on finding our bliss, it is easier to get into alignment with prosperity. What did you do today that brought you bliss?

_____
_____
_____
_____
_____
_____
_____

Week 6

Date _____

How am I already prosperous? What am I thankful for in my life right now?

_____
_____
_____
_____
_____

My prosperity plan!! Write down what you plan to accomplish this week based on what you said you waned to achieve. (Yes, you must write it again. Repetition drives it deeper into your brain. Refine the details if necessary.)

_____
_____
_____
_____
_____
_____
_____
_____
_____
_____

> The first step toward success is taken when you refuse to be a captive of the environment in which you first find yourself.
>
> Mark Caine

Small action steps I took today

1. _____

2. _____

3. _____

action taking meter

I did everything I set out to do

I didn't do anything

Bliss Points
When we focus ourselves on finding our bliss, it is easier to get into alignment with prosperity. What did you do today that brought you bliss?

_____

Week 6

Date _____

How am I already prosperous? What am I thankful for in my life right now?

_____
_____
_____
_____
_____

My prosperity plan!! Write down what you plan to accomplish this week based on what you said you waned to achieve. (Yes, you must write it again. Repetition drives it deeper into your brain. Refine the details if necessary.)

_____
_____
_____
_____
_____
_____
_____
_____
_____
_____

> You cannot climb the ladder of success dressed in the costume of failure.
>
> Zig Ziglar

Small action steps I took today
1. _____

2. _____

3. _____

action taking meter

I did everything I set out to do

I didn't do anything

Bliss Points
When we focus ourselves on finding our bliss, it is easier to get into alignment with prosperity. What did you do today that brought you bliss?

_____

Week 6

Date _____

How am I already prosperous? What am I thankful for in my life right now?

_____
_____
_____
_____
_____

My prosperity plan!! Write down what you plan to accomplish this week based on what you said you waned to achieve. (Yes, you must write it again. Repetition drives it deeper into your brain. Refine the details if necessary.)

_____
_____
_____
_____
_____
_____
_____
_____
_____

> A successful man is one who can lay a firm foundation with the bricks others have thrown at him.
>
> David Brinkley

Small action steps I took today

1. _____
_____
_____

2. _____
_____
_____

3. _____
_____
_____
_____
_____

action taking meter

I did everything I set out to do

I didn't do anything

Bliss Points
When we focus ourselves on finding our bliss, it is easier to get into alignment with prosperity. What did you do today that brought you bliss?

_____
_____
_____
_____
_____
_____
_____
_____
_____
_____
_____
_____

Week 6

Date _____

How am I already prosperous? What am I thankful for in my life right now?

_____
_____
_____
_____
_____

My prosperity plan!! Write down what you plan to accomplish this week based on what you said you waned to achieve. (Yes, you must write it again. Repetition drives it deeper into your brain. Refine the details if necessary.)

_____
_____
_____
_____
_____
_____
_____
_____
_____
_____

> Do you wish to rise?
> Begin by descending.
> You plan a tower that will pierce the clouds?
> Lay first the foundation of humility.
>
> Saint Augustine

Small action steps I took today

1. _____
   _____

2. _____
   _____

3. _____
   _____
   _____
   _____

action taking meter

I did everything I set out to do

⸽⸽⸽⸽⸽⸽⸽⸽⸽⸽⸽⸽⸽⸽⸽⸽⸽⸽
⸽   ⸽
⸽   ⸽
⸽   ⸽
⸽   ⸽
⸽   ⸽
⸽⸽⸽⸽⸽⸽⸽⸽⸽⸽⸽⸽⸽⸽⸽⸽⸽⸽

I didn't do anything

Bliss Points

When we focus ourselves on finding our bliss, it is easier to get into alignment with prosperity. What did you do today that brought you bliss?

_____
_____
_____
_____
_____
_____
_____
_____
_____
_____

Week 6

Date _____

How am I already prosperous? What am I thankful for in my life right now?

_____
_____
_____
_____
_____

My prosperity plan!! Write down what you plan to accomplish this week based on what you said you waned to achieve. (Yes, you must write it again. Repetition drives it deeper into your brain. Refine the details if necessary.)

_____
_____
_____
_____
_____
_____
_____
_____
_____
_____
_____

> Success usually comes to those who are too busy to be looking for it.
>
> Henry David Thoreau

Small action steps I took today

1. _____
   _____
   _____

2. _____
   _____
   _____

3. _____
   _____
   _____
   _____

action taking meter

I did
everything I
set out to do

I didn't do
anything

Bliss Points

When we focus ourselves on finding our bliss, it is easier to get into alignment with prosperity. What did you do today that brought you bliss?

_____
_____
_____
_____
_____
_____
_____
_____
_____
_____
_____
_____

What a week! I love my prosperity journal.

Write down the difference you notice in your life as you have been focused on
prosperity.

> The only place success comes before work is in the dictionary.
>
> Vince Lombardi

**** *Blissful Actions* ****

Date _____

Weekly Check-In

Have I been staying in alignment with my values during my prosperity practice? Have I been using my strengths to the best of my ability? Have I been seeking help when I need it? Am I staying authentic to myself?

_____
_____
_____
_____
_____
_____
_____
_____
_____
_____
_____
_____
_____
_____
_____
_____
_____

prosperity meter

Life's great, but..I'm ready for more.

I am thriving!! Life is blooming.

Week 7

Date _____

How am I already prosperous? What abilities do I have to contribute to my prosperity?

_____
_____
_____
_____
_____
_____

My prosperity plan!! Write down what you plan to accomplish this week based on what you said you wanted to achieve.

_____
_____
_____
_____
_____
_____
_____
_____
_____

Big actions I need to take this week in accordance with my plan.

_____
_____
_____
_____
_____
_____
_____

Small action steps I took today

1. _____
_____
_____

2. _____
_____
_____

3. _____
_____
_____

action taking meter

I did everything I set out to do

I didn't do anything

> I don't know of any entrepreneurs who have achieved any level of success without persistence and determination.
>
> Harvey Mackay

Bliss Points
When we focus ourselves on finding our bliss, it is easier to get into alignment with prosperity. What did you do today that brought you bliss?

_____
_____
_____
_____
_____
_____
_____

Week 7

Date _____

How am I already prosperous? What am I thankful for in my life right now?

_____
_____
_____
_____
_____

My prosperity plan!! Write down what you plan to accomplish this week based on what you said you waned to achieve. (Yes, you must write it again. Repetition drives it deeper into your brain. Refine the details if necessary.)

_____
_____
_____
_____
_____
_____
_____
_____
_____
_____

> The difference between a successful person and others is not a lack of strength, not a lack of knowledge, but rather a lack of will.
>
> — Vince Lombardi

Small action steps I took today

1. _____

2. _____

3. _____

action taking meter

I did everything I set out to do

I didn't do anything

Bliss Points
When we focus ourselves on finding our bliss, it is easier to get into alignment with prosperity. What did you do today that brought you bliss?

Week 7

Date _____

How am I already prosperous? What am I thankful for in my life right now?

_____
_____
_____
_____
_____

My prosperity plan!! Write down what you plan to accomplish this week based on what you said you waned to achieve. (Yes, you must write it again. Repetition drives it deeper into your brain. Refine the details if necessary.)

_____
_____
_____
_____
_____
_____
_____
_____
_____
_____
_____

> You might well remember that nothing can bring you success but yourself.
>
> Napoleon Hill

Small action steps I took today

1. _____

2. _____

3. _____

action taking meter

I did everything I set out to do

I didn't do anything

Bliss Points
When we focus ourselves on finding our bliss, it is easier to get into alignment with prosperity. What did you do today that brought you bliss?

Week 7

Date _____

How am I already prosperous? What am I thankful for in my life right now?

_____
_____
_____
_____

My prosperity plan!! Write down what you plan to accomplish this week based on what you said you waned to achieve. (Yes, you must write it again. Repetition drives it deeper into your brain. Refine the details if necessary.)

_____
_____
_____
_____
_____
_____
_____
_____
_____
_____
_____

> If one advances confdently in the direction of his dreams, and endeavors to live the life which he has imagined, he will meet with a success unexpected in common hours.
>
> Henry David Throeau

Small action steps I took today

1. _____
_____
_____

2. _____
_____
_____

3. _____
_____
_____
_____

action taking meter

I did everything I set out to do

⋮

I didn't do anything

Bliss Points

When we focus ourselves on finding our bliss, it is easier to get into alignment with prosperity. What did you do today that brought you bliss?

_____
_____
_____
_____
_____
_____
_____
_____
_____
_____
_____
_____

Week 7

Date _____

How am I already prosperous? What am I thankful for in my life right now?

_____
_____
_____
_____
_____

My prosperity plan!! Write down what you plan to accomplish this week based on what you said you waned to achieve. (Yes, you must write it again. Repetition drives it deeper into your brain. Refine the details if necessary.)

_____
_____
_____
_____
_____
_____
_____
_____
_____
_____
_____

> If you work just for money, you'll never make it, but if you love what you're doing and you always put the customer first, success will be yours.
>
> Ray Kroc

Small action steps I took today

1. _____

2. _____

3. _____

action taking meter

I did everything I set out to do

I didn't do anything

Bliss Points

When we focus ourselves on finding our bliss, it is easier to get into alignment with prosperity. What did you do today that brought you bliss?

Week 7

Date _____

How am I already prosperous? What am I thankful for in my life right now?

_____
_____
_____
_____

My prosperity plan!! Write down what you plan to accomplish this week based on what you said you waned to achieve. (Yes, you must write it again. Repetition drives it deeper into your brain. Refine the details if necessary.)

_____
_____
_____
_____
_____
_____
_____
_____
_____
_____
_____

> Before you can become a millionaire, you must learn to think like one. You must learn how to motivate yourself to counter fear with courage.
>
> — Thomas J. Stanley

Small action steps I took today

1. _____
_____
_____

2. _____
_____
_____

3. _____
_____
_____
_____
_____

action taking meter

I did everything I set out to do

[ ]

I didn't do anything

Bliss Points

When we focus ourselves on finding our bliss, it is easier to get into alignment with prosperity. What did you do today that brought you bliss?

_____
_____
_____
_____
_____
_____
_____
_____
_____
_____
_____

What a week! I love my prosperity journal.

Write down the difference you notice in your life as you have been focused on prosperity.

_____
_____
_____
_____
_____
_____
_____
_____

> The way a team plays as a whole determines its success. You may have the greatest bunch of individual stars in the world, but if they don't play together, the club won't be worth a dime.
>
> Babe Ruth

**** *Blissful Actions* ****

_____
_____
_____
_____
_____

Date _____

Weekly Check-In

Have I been staying in alignment with my values during my prosperity practice? Have I been using my strengths to the best of my ability? Have I been seeking help when I need it? Am I staying authentic to myself?

_____
_____
_____
_____
_____
_____
_____
_____
_____
_____
_____
_____
_____
_____
_____
_____
_____
_____
_____

prosperity meter

| Life's great, but..I'm ready for more. | | I am thriving!! Life is blooming. |

Week 8

Date _____

How am I already prosperous? What abilities do I have to contribute to my prosperity?

_____
_____
_____
_____
_____
_____

My prosperity plan!! Write down what you plan to accomplish this week based on what you said you wanted to achieve.

_____
_____
_____
_____
_____
_____
_____
_____

Big actions I need to take this week in accordance with my plan.

_____
_____
_____
_____
_____
_____
_____

Small action steps I took today

1. _____
_____
_____

2. _____
_____
_____

3. _____
_____
_____

action taking meter

I did everything I set out to do

I didn't do anything

> There is nothing more difficult to take in hand, more perilous to conduct, or more uncertain in its success, than to take the lead in the introduction of a new order of things.
> Niccolo Machiavelli

Bliss Points
When we focus ourselves on finding our bliss, it is easier to get into alignment with prosperity. What did you do today that brought you bliss?

_____
_____
_____
_____
_____
_____
_____

Week 8

Date _____

How am I already prosperous? What am I thankful for in my life right now?

_____
_____
_____
_____
_____

My prosperity plan!! Write down what you plan to accomplish this week based on what you said you waned to achieve. (Yes, you must write it again. Repetition drives it deeper into your brain. Refine the details if necessary.)

_____
_____
_____
_____
_____
_____
_____
_____
_____
_____
_____

> If you want to succeed you should strike out on new paths, rather than travel the worn paths of accepted success.
>
> John D. Rockefeller

Small action steps I took today

1. _____

_____

2. _____

_____

3. _____

_____

_____

_____

action taking meter

I did everything I set out to do

I didn't do anything

Bliss Points
When we focus ourselves on finding our bliss, it is easier to get into alignment with prosperity. What did you do today that brought you bliss?

_____
_____
_____
_____
_____
_____
_____
_____
_____
_____
_____
_____
_____

Week 8

Date _____

How am I already prosperous? What am I thankful for in my life right now?

_____
_____
_____
_____

My prosperity plan!! Write down what you plan to accomplish this week based on what you said you waned to achieve. (Yes, you must write it again. Repetition drives it deeper into your brain. Refine the details if necessary.)

_____
_____
_____
_____
_____
_____
_____
_____
_____
_____

> The path to success is to take massive, determined action.
>
> Tony Robbins

Small action steps I took today

1. _____
   _____
   _____

2. _____
   _____
   _____

3. _____
   _____
   _____
   _____

action taking meter

I did everything I set out to do

I didn't do anything

Bliss Points
When we focus ourselves on finding our bliss, it is easier to get into alignment with prosperity. What did you do today that brought you bliss?

_____
_____
_____
_____
_____
_____
_____
_____
_____
_____
_____

Week 8

Date _____

How am I already prosperous? What am I thankful for in my life right now?

_____
_____
_____
_____
_____

My prosperity plan!! Write down what you plan to accomplish this week based on what you said you waned to achieve. (Yes, you must write it again. Repetition drives it deeper into your brain. Refine the details if necessary.)

_____
_____
_____
_____
_____
_____
_____
_____
_____
_____
_____

> Seventy percent of success in life is showing up.
>
> Woody Allen

Small action steps I took today

1. _____
   _____
   _____

2. _____
   _____
   _____

3. _____
   _____
   _____
   _____
   _____

action taking meter

I did everything I set out to do

I didn't do anything

Bliss Points

When we focus ourselves on finding our bliss, it is easier to get into alignment with prosperity. What did you do today that brought you bliss?

_____
_____
_____
_____
_____
_____
_____
_____
_____
_____
_____
_____

Week 8

Date _____

How am I already prosperous? What am I thankful for in my life right now?

_____
_____
_____
_____

My prosperity plan!! Write down what you plan to accomplish this week based on what you said you waned to achieve. (Yes, you must write it again. Repetition drives it deeper into your brain. Refine the details if necessary.)

_____
_____
_____
_____
_____
_____
_____
_____
_____

> The season of failure is the best time for sowing the seeds of success.
>
> Paramahansa Yogananda

Small action steps I took today

1. _____

2. _____

3. _____

action taking meter

I did everything I set out to do

I didn't do anything

Bliss Points
When we focus ourselves on finding our bliss, it is easier to get into alignment with prosperity. What did you do today that brought you bliss?

_____

Week 8

Date _____

How am I already prosperous? What am I thankful for in my life right now?

_____
_____
_____
_____
_____

My prosperity plan!! Write down what you plan to accomplish this week based on what you said you waned to achieve. (Yes, you must write it again. Repetition drives it deeper into your brain. Refine the details if necessary.)

_____
_____
_____
_____
_____
_____
_____
_____
_____
_____
_____

> A champion is afraid of losing. Everyone else is afraid of winning.
>
> Billie Jean King

Small action steps I took today

1. _____
_____
_____

2. _____
_____
_____

3. _____
_____
_____
_____

action taking meter

I did everything I set out to do

I didn't do anything

Bliss Points
When we focus ourselves on finding our bliss, it is easier to get into alignment with prosperity. What did you do today that brought you bliss?

_____
_____
_____
_____
_____
_____
_____
_____
_____
_____
_____
_____

What a week! I love my prosperity journal.

Write down the difference you notice in your life as you have been focused on prosperity.

_____
_____
_____
_____
_____
_____
_____

> The five essential entrepreneurial skills for success: Concentration, Discrimination, Organization, Innovation and Communication.
>
> Harold S. Geneen

**** *Blissful Actions* ****

_____
_____
_____
_____

Date _____

Weekly Check-In

Have I been staying in alignment with my values during my prosperity practice? Have I been using my strengths to the best of my ability? Have I been seeking help when I need it? Am I staying authentic to myself?

prosperity meter

Life's great, but..I'm ready for more.

I am thriving!! Life is blooming.

prosperous perceptions, realizations, and notes

prosperous perceptions, realizations, and notes

prosperous perceptions, realizations, and notes

prosperous perceptions, realizations, and notes

prosperous perceptions, realizations, and notes

Available Now From Uiri Press

The I Am So Happy journal is a 46 day exploration into what makes you happy.

By Sky Hawk
ISBN 978-0-9979051-0-6

The I Am So Grateful journal is a 35 day voyage into bringing more thankfulness into your life.

By Sky Hawk
ISBN 978-0-9979051-1-3

The I am So Peaceful journal is an expedition into what brings peace into your life and what you can do to keep it there.

By Sky Hawk
ISBN 978-0-9979051-2-0

About the Author

Sky Hawk is an author, artist, nature lover, successful entrepreneur, healer, and mother. She is the creator of her life, the I Am So series, herbal tracking journals, and much more. She helps people feel the love in themselves and is a spreader of joy.
Visit her and follow along the journey
website: SkyTheAuthor.com
facebook: @skyhawkauthor
instagram: sky_hawk_author